THE NEXT TWELVE DAYS
OF YOUR NEW LIFE

"The Next Twelve Days of Your New Life"

Written by David Shannon Wooten

Cover design and art: Amanda Wipperman
Editor: Stacy Click

ISBN: 978-0-578-67015-7

Your best days are ahead of you.

Jeremiah 29:11, *"For I know the plans I have for you,"
declares the LORD, "plans to prosper you and not to harm
you, plans to give you hope and a future."*

CONTENTS

The Believer's Prayer   i

A Word of Encouragement   iii

Day 1   A Whole New World   1
Day 2   A Tree Doesn't Produce Fruit Overnight   3
Day 3   Who's Talking to Me?   5
Day 4   Maps Will Show You the Way   9
Day 5   A Conversation with God   13
Day 6   Friends That are Going in the Same Direction   17
Day 7   Church: Is it Really That Important?   21
Day 8   What's the Big Deal with Small Groups?   23
Day 9   Something Very Valuable Within You   27
Day 10   Going Public   29
Day 11   Don't Forget to Refuel   33
Day 12   Determination: The One Thing You Must Possess   35

Powerful Prayers That Make a Difference   37

Someone to Call   41

The Believer's Prayer

Romans 10:9, "If you declare with your mouth, 'Jesus is Lord,' and believe in your heart that God raised him from the dead, you will be saved."

As you sincerely believe, pray the following prayer out loud. You are declaring that Jesus is your Savior, and He is faithful to begin a new work in your heart and life.

Dear Heavenly Father, thank You for sending your Son, Jesus who died on the cross for me. I believe He took my sins. I believe You raised Him from the dead. So, with my heart and with my mouth I confess Jesus Christ is my Lord. I surrender everything to Him. I follow Him and I thank you for saving me. I receive what You did for me. I am Saved in Jesus' name, Amen.

A Word Of Encouragement

Congratulations on your decision to receive Jesus Christ as your Savior. Throughout your life, you will discover how this decision is THE MOST important decision you will EVER make. I'm so happy for you and excited for you to experience all that Jesus will bring into your life.

While you will have some challenges ahead of you, you will also experience incredible moments and seasons in your life. I pray this book will help answer some of your questions, give guidance and encourage you for the next twelve days.

Your next twelve days are important for your success as a Christ-Follower. The consistency of thinking, reflecting, devoting some time in prayer and reading a few verses in the Bible will be an incredible help to you. Take just a few moments each day to read these short thoughts about these important questions and topics. I have selected twelve topics that I feel are the most influential in your life at this moment.

I believe in you! I believe in the faithfulness of Jesus working in you.

Shannon D. Wooten
Lead Pastor
Newspring Church

Day 1: A Whole New World

We hear a lot of statements in church that we may not fully understand, like "saved." What does, "I'm saved" mean?

Saved simply means that we acknowledge we were sinners, lost, without hope and disconnected from God. We were unsure about our life after this life. We now know that God loves us so much that He sent His Son, Jesus, to give His life for us. We understand that Jesus willingly died for our sins so that we can find forgiveness. No one could ever live good enough to earn Salvation. Only Jesus was perfect enough to become the Savior for humanity. He took our place on the cross to forgive our sins, give us freedom, and have eternal life. We now believe and confess Jesus Christ as our Savior. We are no longer lost but found. Not only are our sins forgiven but we are cleansed from sin. We are no longer in bondage to sin but live in freedom and in the abundant life that Jesus gives.

Now you are saved and a whole new world is open to you. God will show you how to live life with purpose and fulfillment. You will discover how to live with power and the grace of God. You will transform into a powerhouse of faith and know real victory.

The best example I can give you of what a whole new world looks like is this: think about the caterpillar. The caterpillar knows life by crawling. The caterpillar views the world from the perspective of crawling in low places. But once the caterpillar goes into a state of metamorphosis, it transforms into a beautiful butterfly. Once a caterpillar that only knew how to crawl, is now a new creation, viewing life at an elevated position. Once crawling, now flying. The butterfly experiences a whole new world.

God will show you different principles of how to live life. You will see love in a whole new way and will view problems and challenges differently. Over time, God will place new desires in you that will guide you to your purpose and fulfillment.

Your willingness, commitment, and surrendering to God is absolutely key to transforming into a whole new creation. A beautiful part of this journey is God promises to always be with you every step of the way.

Scriptures to Study:
- Romans 3:22-26
- John 3:16
- Romans 5:8
- 2 Corinthians 5:17

Prayer:
Father, I permit You to open my eyes to a whole new perspective and a way to see the world. Let me see the way You see. Place new desires within me. Give me wisdom and insight into Your Word. Transform me into the person You desire me to be. Help me reach my full potential for the purpose You created me.

Day 2: A Tree Doesn't Produce Fruit Overnight

I'm always encouraging people not to be discouraged when they don't see changes in their lives right away. I get it, we all want quick results, and we don't want to struggle with sin, addictions, or behaviors that we know are hindering our lives.

It is a misconception to think Christians are supposed to be instantly perfect and will never sin. Yes, it is God's desire for us to remove sinful behaviors from our lives. However, we must understand this will take time, and it demands His help. Becoming like Christ is a gradual process. You must fully understand that making a mistake does not make you unsaved. God still loves you the same. God will help you grow and overcome temptation or weaknesses.

Remember, a fruit tree does not bear fruit overnight. There's a process to its growth. Someone plants a seed and applies water to the seed regularly. The seed will sprout and project out of the ground; the sunlight is necessary for its growth. Nutrients are added to the soil to nourish its health. Days, weeks, months, and years pass before one piece of fruit is evident. Like the seed, when you gave your life to Christ, God planted you. Your daily relationship with Christ is growing as a result of the investments you are making daily. Your investments toward your relationship with Christ are what is nourishing you, causing your faith to grow.

Just like the tree needs good soil, water, and sunlight, you too are creating an environment conducive for spiritual growth. The time you spend in God's Word is watering your faith, causing it to grow. Intentionally having conversations with God in prayer and taking moments to worship Him is bringing you into His presence. His presence is like the required sunlight for the tree. Think of your prayer and worship as SONlight.

Don't get discouraged if you make a mistake or sin. God does not want you to run from Him. He wants you to run to Him and ask for His help. The Bible instructs us to come to Him, admit where we messed up, and He is faithful to forgive us. Repeating these steps is part of the process of growth. Before you know it, you will not struggle in the same areas. You will become strong in faith and move to other areas of your life that are even more productive.

Scriptures to Study:
- 1 John 1:8-10
- Luke 17:5
- 1 Peter 2:2-3
- Colossians 1:9-10

Prayer:
Father, help me to be patient. When I feel I am not making progress, remind me that growth is taking place within me. Please give me the desire to bring the right things into my life that will help me grow in my faith. Give me the strength and wisdom to change behaviors and habits that will contribute to producing the right kind of fruit in my life.

Day 3: Who's Talking To Me?

There's a lot of noise in our world today. We are constantly flooded with so many voices, infomercials, advertisements, and advice, not to mention the news that seems to be mostly negative.

A one-hour tv show has approximately sixteen minutes of commercials. When you go to the movies, the movie may start at 6:00 p.m. but the first fifteen minutes are filled with trailers designed to attract you to the next great movie. Every phone app has a notification that sends a tone or vibration that contends for our attention. They interrupt our focus, thoughts, and conversations.

We often think that people who hear voices are crazy and will eventually end up in straitjackets and analyzed by people in white coats. But the truth is every one of us hears different voices in our lives; media outlets, our family, our friends, and even our thoughts. They all speak to us.

You must pay close attention to the voices you hear because whatever grabs your attention will grab your focus. Eventually, it will capture your heart.

We can become persuaded by the voices we allow to speak to us. This is not always bad if the voice is leading us in the right direction. But if these voices are in direct opposition to the way God is leading you, then it can be devastating.

Identify Four Voices

Four notable voices continually speak to us in our thoughts. These are the voices of:

- God
- Demons
- Others
- Yourself

God will give you the wisdom to identify which voice is speaking to you. Once you know which voice is talking to you, you will know what to do with the message you are receiving. The most important step you can take is to evaluate if the voice you are hearing agrees with what the Bible says.

Every new Believer will eventually hear a voice that will tell them they are not saved. But that statement does not agree with what God says in His Word. So that voice must be ignored.

As you continue to read the Bible, you will develop an ear for God's voice. It's like speaking to someone that you know very well on the phone. You may not be able to see their face, but you have talked with them so many times before, you know their voice. The same with God. The more you spend time with Him, the more you will know His voice. Jesus said in His Word, "My sheep know my voice and another they will not follow."

Scriptures to Study:
- John 10:5, 27
- Romans 10:17

Prayer:
Father, give me discernment to know which voice is speaking to me. Please give me the wisdom to listen to

the right voices that surround me. Give me influences that will help increase my faith, encouragement, and joy. Please help me to be open to influences that will instruct me and add value to my life.

Day 4: Maps Will Show You the Way

If you want to go to Disney World and you live in Cincinnati, Ohio, you do not want to head north on I75. You will eventually end up in Detroit, Michigan, nowhere near the Big Mouse and all the fun stuff. If you have been driving for a few years, you have probably used the Maps app on your phone or a GPS. If you're not sure which direction to take, getting direction from those resources is wise and saves you a lot of stress.

When we are driving, we pay attention to road signs, the specifics of an address, and the direction of north, south, east, or west. Receiving the right information and having the knowledge of which direction to go will ensure success for your journey.

The same is true in living our lives. We make decisions every day. Some of those decisions are life-changing. The key to making significant decisions is making sure we are well informed and able to perceive the outcome of a choice.

The Bible is our "Maps" app for making decisions in life. God has placed principles in the Bible that give wisdom for decision making.

The Bible says God's Word is a lamp to our feet and a light to our path. Notice the Bible mentions feet and path explicitly. The principles found in the Bible will give direction for each step; each decision you need to make. The principles will also help you perceive which direction each choice will take you in your future.

If you want a good idea where you will be five to ten years from now, pay close attention to the choices you are making today. God promises us that if we follow His Word, we will have success.

Choose a Bible translation that is easy to read and understand. Many excellent translations will help you learn the Bible. NIV, NLT, NKJV, and The Message Bible are a few excellent translations that use today's language to translate God's message to you. You can also download the YouVersion Bible app on your phone. This app will help you have easy access to daily scriptures, short devotionals, and it will even play an audio file of the scriptures. Listening to the Bible is an excellent option while driving to and from work.

I want to encourage you to first read 1, 2, 3 John in the New Testament. They are short but powerful chapters that communicate the heart of God. Then read the first four books of the New Testament. Matthew, Mark, Luke, and John will give you four perspectives of the birth, life, miracles, death, and resurrection of Jesus.

The Bible is not only necessary to navigate our lives, but is also referred to as the essential food for us. Just like your natural body needs natural food to survive, your soul and spirit need to eat as well. Reading and reflecting on the Scriptures feeds your soul and spirit.

Reading the Word of God will increase your faith. Following the instructions of God's Word will give your life direction that will lead to real success and fulfillment.

Scriptures to Study:
- Psalm 119:104-106
- Deuteronomy 5:33

- Joshua 1:8
- 1 Peter 2:2
- Romans 10:17

Prayer:

Father, lead and guide me by Your Holy Spirit. Your Word is a lamp to my feet and a light to my path. I give the Holy Spirit permission to nudge me in the right direction and convict me where I may be getting off course. I need to follow the plan and purpose that You have for my life. My heart and mind are open to Your Word, giving me guidance in every area of my life.

Day 5: A Conversation With God

Is there someone in your life who is easy to talk to? Someone who has wisdom and who gives excellent advice? Someone who would never steer you in the wrong direction? Someone who you know loves you and wants the very best for you? It is probably easy for you to share your heart with them.

Praying to God is the same as having a natural conversation with someone who loves you, desires the best for you, and will never turn you away. Prayer is sometimes viewed as only a religious activity; it must be accomplished on our knees, with eyes closed, only at church, and most of the time, it is perceived to be very tiresome. This is a huge misconception.

I want you to see prayer as merely having a conversation with God. You openly and honestly share your heart with Him and listen for Him to share His heart with you. More than likely, you will not hear an audible voice in return. God speaks to you through your innermost being and your conscience. You will have an impression, a thought, and you will know it is His voice because what you hear will align with the Bible.

Like a father who loves to talk and spend time with his children, God anticipates having a conversation with you. Prayer is God's idea. He designed prayer as a way to connect with Him.

Think about it. You and I have access to the Creator of the Universe. He has all the answers, all the resources, and has incredible abilities! You and I have DIRECT access to Him through prayer!

When you are hurting, God is there to comfort you with His presence in prayer. When you are lonely, He is there to assure you He is always with you and will never abandon you. When you are in need, He simply invites you to ask Him for His help.

The following is a suitable format you can use to help you spend time in prayer:

1. Praise | Words of love and appreciation to God.
2. Silent Surrender | Give Him your heart, life, and full attention.
3. Confession | Inner cleansing.
4. Scripture Praying | Prayers inspired by the Scripture verses in the Bible.
5. Watching | Developing alertness of what is affecting your faith and soul.
6. Intercession | Pray for those who need to commit their life to Jesus.
7. Petition | Express your personal needs or the needs of others.
8. Thanksgiving | Express how grateful you are for God's blessings.
9. Singing | Worship God in song.
10. Meditation | Reflect on certain Scriptures that come to your mind.
11. Listening | Receive instruction, encouragement, affirmation from God. While you are in prayer, listen to your thoughts that may be prompted by God.
12. Praise | Words of love and appreciation to God.

Scriptures to Study:
- Jeremiah 33:3

- Psalm 100:4
- 1 John 5:14
- James 5:16

Prayer:
    Father, I desire to talk with You every day. I recognize that Your counsel is more important than any other advice in this world. Today I share my thoughts, hurt, concerns, needs, and the things that bring me joy with You. I know You are listening to my prayer and in return, You are speaking to me. Thank You for hearing me and answering my prayer.

Day 6: Friends That Are Going In The Same Direction

It is in our human DNA to learn from one another. As children, we learn and adopt behaviors from our parents, siblings, and close friends. Our success is determined by who we allow to influence us.

As a teen growing up, I was told this statement by coaches, teachers, pastors, and other mentors, "Show me your friends, and I will show you your future." As time has passed and I have made a lot of mistakes and have seen some success, I can tell you this is more than a statement; it is a life principle.

Proverbs 13:20 gives us wise instruction that "he who walks with the wise grows wise, but a companion of fools suffers harm." The Bible also informs us, "Do not be misled: 'Bad company corrupts good character'" (1 Corinthians 15:33).

Think about the power of a magnet. A magnet can magnetize other pieces of metal by constant contact and rubbing that piece of metal in a specific direction.

The people we hang with, share our feelings with, ask advice from, or attempt to get approval from, have the potential to shape our behaviors, the way we think and even help form our belief system. We would be wise to ensure that the people we share life with are people who are going in the same direction that God wants us to go.

God will help bring good friends into our lives, but we have to be willing to associate with people who are intentional about growing in their faith and developing their relationship with God.

Developing friendships at church, connecting with other Christians at work or school, joining Bible studies, or participating in activities where there are other Christians will significantly contribute to your success in growing in your faith.

The Bible uses the illustration as a piece of metal that can sharpen another piece of metal. "As iron sharpens iron, so a friend sharpens a friend" (Proverbs 27:17). There are two fundamental principles here in this truth: 1.) The iron, or the friends, must connect. 2.) Their substance and how they connect will determine if they will sharpen one another or dull one another.

Whom we connect with will determine what we learn. Our friends play a massive role in shaping our future.

Ask God to connect you with people who will add value to your spiritual life.

Scriptures to Study:
- Ecclesiastes 4:9-10
- Proverbs 18:24
- Proverbs 11:14
- 1 Thessalonians 5:11

Prayer:
Father, I realize the influences in my life are integral to the development of my faith. Give me the favor to acquire godly relationships. Help me to discern which relationships may be toxic to my faith. Give me wisdom to know which relationships I will need to let go

or at least limit. Use me to help someone in their faith journey.

Day 7: Church: Is It Really That Important?

Let's make it clear; going to church will not make you a Christian, just like standing in a garage won't transform you into a car. Church attendance will not earn you Salvation and it does not replace or become a substitute for your relationship with Jesus.

The question often asked, "is attending church, belonging to a church, or getting involved in a church, really that important?" That is a great question! Some people do not even ask the question, they just state what they believe, "Jesus saved me, and I don't need the church. I only need Jesus." "If I don't go to church, it doesn't mean I'm not a Christian. I still love Jesus." Another statement I have heard is, "I love Jesus, I just don't like church."

I understand these statements. However, it is highly essential to bring clarity to why the church exists and what its purpose is.

First, we must understand the church is God's idea. The church is not a building, it's not an organization, and it's not a denomination. The church is people. God is the one who created the church.

Second, the church is God's answer to reach the world with the Good News that Jesus has come so all can experience His Salvation. There is no plan B for sharing Jesus with the world. God not only created the church, but He also gave the church an incredible purpose and mission.

Third, God views the church as one big family. There are many Scriptures in the Bible that refer to the church as the "family of God." Every member of the family has a specific gift, skill, and purpose. When we come together, we have incredible power, and we are more productive than when we are alone.

Sunday morning worship is vital in strengthening our faith and relationship with Jesus. It's the one time each week that we can be in the presence of our "spiritual family" and worship God together. God designed our spiritual growth to connect to others. Worshipping together as one family is significant to God.

Think about how important it is for families to get together for "family" meals. So many great things happen around the family table as a meal is shared. A stronger sense of unity and closeness happens through conversation and bonding when the family comes together.

Scriptures to Study:
- Ephesians 4:11-13
- Ephesians 5:29-30
- Colossians 3:16

Prayer:
Father, help me see Your church as Your Body and not just a building or organization. I thank You that You move through Your church and use people to help further Your mission. I know Your church is not perfect, however, You use imperfect people. As I engage in worship and receive Biblical teaching from Your church, I pray my faith and relationship will grow with You and with others.

Day 8: What's The Big Deal With Small Groups?

As I stated on Day 7, a Sunday, Saturday or Friday church service is vital to your spiritual growth. It's not just a bunch of hyper people in one room singing and listening to preaching. It's much deeper than that. It's God's people, Believers, coming together in unity to worship and learn from God's Word. It has a spiritual dynamic and a purpose to fulfill in our lives.

However, Sunday morning worship can only fulfill a portion of our spiritual growth. A huge part of our spiritual growth comes with connecting with other Believers who are growing in their faith in small groups. When I say "small group," I'm referring to any group that has elements of Scripture reading and devotional studies. Even groups that meet to participate in activities like biking, walking, golfing, serving and countless other activities could be considered small groups. These groups meet and share Scripture verses as a devotional and, for ten to twenty minutes, discuss how the Scripture relates to their personal life and their spiritual growth.

Some churches will title them Life Groups, Small Groups, Bible Studies, Sunday School Class, Connect Groups, or just simply Groups. Whatever the title may be, these small groups represent how the first church in history was formed and would function. You can read this in the book of Acts. They met in homes, churches, or even in the marketplace. Yes, the first church would meet in a larger church service, but they also met in smaller groups.

The big deal with small groups is you can ask questions, you can share your experience and thoughts, and most importantly, you can develop relationships with other Believers. There is incredible strength in relationships.

To illustrate the power of relationships, consider a flock of geese. God created and designed geese to be in a relationship. Look at these powerful lessons.

Lesson 1: As each goose flaps its wings, it creates an "uplift" for the birds that follow. By flying in a "V" formation, the whole flock adds 71% greater flying range than if each bird flew alone.

People who share a common direction and sense of community can get where they are going quicker and easier because they are traveling on the thrust of one another.

Lesson 2: When a goose falls out of formation, it suddenly feels the drag and resistance of flying alone. It quickly moves back into formation to take advantage of the lifting power of the bird in front of it.

If we have as much common sense as a goose, we will stay in formation with those headed where we want to go. We are willing to accept their help and give our support to others in return.

Lesson 3: When the lead goose tires, it rotates back into the formation and another goose flies to the point position.

It pays to take turns doing the hard tasks and sharing leadership. As with geese, people are interdependent, have different capabilities, and have unique arrangements of gifts, talents, or resources.

Lesson 4: Geese flying in formation honk to encourage those up front to keep up their speed.
We need to make sure our "honking" is encouraging. In groups where there is encouragement, the production is much higher. The power of encouragement (to stand by

one's heart or core values and encourage the heart and core of others) is the quality of honking we seek.

Lesson 5: When a goose gets sick, wounded, or shot down, two geese drop out of formation and follow it down to help protect it. They stay with it until it dies or can fly again. Then they launch out with another formation or catch up with the flock.

We can learn the lesson from geese to stand by each other in difficult times as well as when we are strong. God designed us for relationships. Good relationships help us to grow in our faith, and it is how we share our experiences with God and others. The entire Kingdom of God is built around relationships. A great place to develop incredible relationships is in a small group at your church.

Scriptures to Study:
- Colossians 3:12-14
- Psalm 133
- Hebrews 10:24-25

Prayer:
Father, I'm asking that You bring me total freedom in my life. Freedom from my past, freedom from hurts, betrayal, addictions, anger, resentment and anything else in my life where You want me to be free. Please give me the courage to join a small group and engage in studying Your Word with other Believers. Please help me to see the importance You have placed on our need for relationships, for encouragement, learning, and spiritual growth.

Day 9: Something Very Valuable Within You

God created you and has placed something valuable within you. Most people do not feel they have value because all they see is their flaws and shortcomings. The devil is very good at highlighting our weaknesses and encouraging thoughts in our heads that make us not feel useful.

God wants you to see and believe you are valuable. And He wants you to understand that what He has placed within you is valuable to others.

The Bible tells us that every good gift comes from God. Your gifts and abilities have been given to you by your Heavenly Father. When we make light or doubt our abilities, we are critical of the gifts that God created within us.

When we look at dirt, mud, or soil, we think of something that needs to be swept off our rugs or washed out of our clothes. But if we take a closer look, the soil is where we find valuable minerals, nutrients, expensive stones, gold, and silver.

The valuable things that God has placed within you must not be mistaken or overlooked. As you honestly evaluate what God has placed within you, you will find He has designed you to use your gifts to help others.

Take some time to do a gift assessment. There are many free assessments that will help you discover your gifts and personality strengths. Newspring Church has a gift assessment that you can take in our Growth Track classes.

Find ways to use your abilities to make an impact on other people. One great way to do this is to get connected to a ministry team at your church. Serving on a ministry team with others can be so rewarding and beneficial in a lot of ways. You will find that using your abilities to serve others will be both beneficial to you and those you serve. There's nothing more satisfying in life than knowing you are living out your God-given purpose.

God loves stewardship and He loves to bless those who give what they have to make a difference in others. When you offer your abilities to serve others, it pleases God, and in return, He brings more blessings into your life.

Using your abilities to serve others is a huge part of the life of a successful Christ-Follower. Don't let the devil talk you out of using the valuable abilities that God has placed within you.

Scriptures to Study:
- Psalm 139:13-16
- Jeremiah 29:11
- Genesis 1:27
- Jeremiah 1:5

Prayer:

Father, I thank You for creating me in Your image. I recognize all gifts come from You. When I am discouraged or feel insignificant, remind me that You are at work within me. I desire to use the gifts and abilities You have given me to help others and to bring You glory.

Day 10: Going Public

Telling your family and friends what Jesus has done in your life will take your experience to another level. We call this "going public." Going public will make a positive impact on the people around you. You are sharing your story and your decision to believe Jesus is your Savior. You are sharing how Jesus has changed your life, how you think, and how you see the world. Just think, your story of what Jesus has done for you will be what someone needs to hear to help them decide to follow Jesus. Your story will sow incredible seeds in the hearts of the people around you. Sharing stories about Jesus is how the entire world will hear and have opportunities to believe in Him.

A Wedding Ring

The first step in going public is choosing Water Baptism. Water Baptism is a public statement that you have committed your life to Christ. It's like a wedding ring between a husband and wife. The ring doesn't make them married, but it is a symbol of their commitment to one another and everyone around them. You are announcing an inward work of Jesus in your life with an outward sign.

A Sign That Your Sins Are Washed Away

Water Baptism is a symbol that your sins have been forgiven and washed away by Jesus.

A Sign of Your New Life

Water Baptism demonstrates 2 Corinthians 5:17, "Therefore, if anyone is in Christ, the new creation has come: The old has gone, the new is here!" Water Baptism is a symbol of Christ's burial and resurrection. Entering the water during Baptism identifies us with Christ's death on the cross, His burial in the tomb, and His resurrection from the dead. *"Going under the water was a burial of your old life; coming up out of it was a resurrection, God raising you from the dead as he did Christ. When you were stuck in your old sin-dead life, you were incapable of responding to God. God brought you alive – right along with Christ! Think of it! All sins forgiven, the slate wiped clean, that old arrest warrant canceled and nailed to Christ's cross"* (Colossians 2:12-14 MSG).

An Act of Faith and Obedience

Water baptism is an act of faith and obedience to the commands of Christ. *"Therefore, go and make disciples of all nations, baptizing them in the name of the Father and of the Son and of the Holy Spirit, and teaching them to obey everything I have commanded you. And surely I am with you always, to the very end of the age"* (Matthew 28:19-20).

Baptism also connects us to the "body of Christ" – his people on Earth. In Baptism, there is a real sense of being joined with other Believers, not just participating in an individual act of our spiritual journey. *"For we were all baptized by one Spirit into one body"* (1 Corinthians 12:12-13).

Take your next step to be baptized in water, and you will deepen your relationship and faith in Christ. Speak to one of the pastors about the next scheduled Water Baptism.

Scriptures to Study:
- Matthew 3:1
- Luke 3:21-22
- Acts 8:35-38
- Romans 6:3-6

Prayer:

Father, give me the boldness to make a public declaration to express the inward work that You have begun in my life. I pray that my Water Baptism will encourage others to decide to commit their life to Jesus. Thank You for forgiving me of my sins. I am so grateful for the new life I have in You.

Day 11: Don't Forget To Refuel

Have you ever run out of fuel in your vehicle? I have a few times. Getting stranded on the side of the road is so frustrating. Today our cars are not only equipped with a fuel gauge, but they also have a computer to estimate how many more miles we can travel on the fuel that is currently in our tank.

Like your vehicle, the experiences we receive as we invest time in God's Word, worship, connecting to God in conversations, and prayer is your spiritual and emotional fuel. We can only go so far on one or two experiences with God. We need to be refueled daily with fresh, new experiences.

Even Jesus, the Son of God, understood the need to refuel daily.

> *"And in the morning, rising up a great while before day, he went out, and departed into a solitary place, and there prayed"* (Mark 1:35).

> *"And when he had sent them away, he departed into a mountain to pray"* (Mark 6:46).

There is no doubt that Jesus carried a heavy load as He regularly ministered to people and faced opposition. Jesus understood that spending time with God in prayer is what gave Him the fuel to stay strong in His faith. Jesus intentionally modeled how to refuel.

You will face struggles and battles that will drain you. Jesus warns Peter that Satan desired to shake him and weaken his faith (Luke 22:31). However, Jesus said, I pray for you that your faith will not fail. As you make it a daily discipline to refuel your soul, God will be faithful to keep you strong.

Ways You Can Refuel
- Spend at least fifteen minutes alone in the morning talking with God. Read at least one Scripture verse every day. The book of Psalms has many encouraging verses that give a reflection on God's power and strength.
- Purchase a devotional book on the topic of growing in your faith, prayer, or about Jesus.
- Listen to a worship song and begin to pray while listening.
- Attend a prayer meeting, small group, Bible study, or worship service. Engage and participate.
- Go on a walk or a run and talk with God.

Scriptures to Study:
- Deuteronomy 4:29

Prayer:
Father, make me aware when my faith is running low. Help me develop excellent daily disciplines that will build reliable faith deposits. Create in me a hunger for Your presence. May I always find strength as I invest time reading Your Word, in conversations with You and in moments of worship. I pray my time of reflection will be insightful and grow my relationship with You.

Day 12: Determination, The One Thing You Must Possess

The Bible has MANY encouraging scriptures that prompt us to be determined, whether we feel like we are winning or failing. Charles Swindoll said, *"Whether you get whipped, or you win, the secret is determining to stay at it."* We see the same attitude communicated with athletes and sports teams. Athletes must learn to condition not only their bodies but also their mind. Hebrews 12:1 says, *"We must be determined to run the race that is before us."* Your life journey is like a race. Paul, the Apostle, used the same analogy in 2 Timothy 4:7-8, *"I have fought the good fight, I have finished the race, and I have remained faithful. And now the prize awaits me—the crown of righteousness, which the Lord, the righteous Judge, will give me on the day of his return. And the prize is not just for me but for all who eagerly look forward to his appearing."* You can hear the determination in his communication. Be determined to be faithful in your commitment to Jesus, and God promises a reward.

Determination is a character trait you will need in your spiritual journey. You will not only have physical obstacles and relationship challenges that will attempt to discourage you, but you will have mental and emotional struggles too. The devil loves to bring doubts, fears, and temptation in areas that will detract our faith and distract our passion for God. However, if you are determined not to quit and not to give up, you will win in the end.

I want to give you a few practical ways you can exercise determination that will help you on your faith journey.

- Be determined to have a conversation with Jesus every day. Listen for Him to speak back to you.
- Be determined to read the Bible, searching for something to speak to you every day. Look for ways to make the Scriptures apply to your life.
- Be determined to connect with other people who are passionate about Jesus.
- Be determined to go to at least one church service every week.
- Be determined to serve God with your skills and abilities. Serving others will develop generosity and eradicate selfishness.
- Be determined to always have hope in God even more so when faced with challenges and discouragement.
- Be always determined to have a joyful heart. Joy is your strength.

Scripture to Study:
- 1 Corinthians 9:24-27

Prayer:

Father, when discouragement comes, remind me to always have hope in You. I resolve in my heart to be determined never to quit or give up my faith. No matter how many times I may fail, I will always get back up and look to You for strength and the restoration of my faith.

Powerful Prayers That Make A Difference

Forgiveness

Father, forgive me of my sins. I desire to obey Your Word. I thank You for giving me wisdom and guidance that helps me stay on the path of righteousness. Place Your desires in my heart. You are faithful to forgive me, and I forgive others who have offended me. I release anger and resentment for those who have hurt me. I pray my release of forgiveness will bring healing.

Stress and Anxiety

Father, grant me the strength to trust You with my life. I proclaim that You are the anchor of my soul. Open my eyes and allow me to see life from Your perspective. I speak Your Word over my soul and emotions. Bring Your tangible presence and Your peace into my mind and soul.

Trust God

Father, I bring to You all of my worries and concerns, knowing you are a good Father who cares about my life. You have a good plan for my life, and I trust that You are leading me in the path You want me to go. I trust that You will bring great opportunities for me. When trouble and challenges come into my life, I believe that You have a great purpose and will make all things work out for good.

Addictions

Father, You are the God who heals and brings breakthroughs. I surrender every addiction to You. Jesus has paid the price on the cross for my victory. It is by His blood that I can stand in victory over every compulsive behavior. I denounce the grip of this addiction and embrace the love of Jesus Christ, who gave His life for me so I can be free. I have complete deliverance and freedom in Jesus Christ.

Finances

Father, You are the one who gives the power to obtain wealth. I ask for Your wisdom and insight to guide me to see an increase in finances. Please help me to exercise discipline to live within my means. I embrace a life of generosity, honoring You with my finances. I'm confident that You will assist me in financial increase and paying off debts as I walk in Your wisdom for financial stewardship.

Marriage

Father, I pray for my marriage to be a reflection of Your glory. Let my relationship with my spouse be as strong as my relationship with You. I pray my love and care for my spouse will continue to grow. Help me to reflect on the kind of love found in 1 Corinthians chapter 13. Please give me the ability to always give support, encouragement, and understanding.

Children

Father, I pray Your grace and favor over my children. I ask for the Holy Spirit to guide them into the purpose You have created for them. I pray their heart and passion will increase for a personal relationship with You. I pray for their health to be sound, physically, and emotionally. I pray for their future spouse and relationships to be equally joined together in their faith.

I pray for favor and success in their career. May they always bring You glory.

Hunger for God

Father, I pray the cares of this world will never decrease or distract my love for You. When temptation causes me to be cold or lukewarm in my passion for You, I give the Holy Spirit permission to prompt my heart. Continue to reveal to me the truths in Your Word. When I come into your presence in worship, I pray Your glory will place a deep hunger within me. I long to know You and experience the joy that You bring.

Holy Spirit

Father, fill me with Your Holy Spirit. I ask for all of the fruit of the Holy Spirit to be evident in my life. I desire to be used in all of the gifts of the Holy Spirit. I understand that the Holy Spirit is the third person of the Trinity. I welcome Him in my life. I seek to be Baptized in the Holy Spirit and desire the prayer language that He gives. I receive the Holy Spirit as my Teacher, Comforter, and Counselor.

Someone To Call

It is vital to have someone to help you on your faith journey. A seasoned Believer, who can help answer questions and pray for you, will give you an incredible advantage in your success. Ask a ministry leader or pastor to connect you with someone who has the heart to see people grow in their faith. You will also be able to find someone at a small group. You can always call the Newspring Church office for assistance. The Newspring Church office phone number is 937-748-0957. You can also go to newspringlive.com for resources to help you grow in your faith.

We would love the opportunity to connect with you on social media. Connect with us on Facebook at Newspring of Springboro and Shannon David Wooten.

ABOUT THE AUTHOR

Shannon Wooten serves as Lead Pastor at Newspring Church in Springboro, Ohio. He has dedicated over 31 years to ministry and loves to help lead people into a growing relationship with Jesus Christ. Shannon is passionate about teaching the Word of God in relevant and practical ways. His direct, practical teaching style helps everyday Believers apply God's truth to relevant issues, relationships and challenges.

www.ingramcontent.com/pod-product-compliance
Lightning Source LLC
Chambersburg PA
CBHW060621030426
42337CB00018B/3137